Getting to Know Our Earth!

By Eliza Webb

Contents

Where is the hottest place on Earth?

Where is the biggest rock on Earth, or the reddest sand?

Get set to learn about these stunning places!

Hot, Hotter, Hottest

This place is **hot**.

The hottest time here is also the wettest time.

It's very humid.

This place is hotter.
It's still hot even when the sun is setting.

This is the hottest place on Earth!

Only the strongest plants live in the hottest place.
These plants like the sun and don't need much water to survive.

Wet, Wetter, Wettest

This place is **wet** most of the time. The bigger the raindrops, the gladder the plants are to get dripped on!

This place is even wetter.
Mist drifts around the hills,
wetting everything.

But it is not the wettest place.

This city is the wettest place on Earth.
Lots of rain is always dropping from the sky.

These big straw hats stop people from getting wet!

Big, Bigger, Biggest

This rock is **big**.

Some brave people hike up it.
Getting to the top is hard!

This cold rock is even bigger.

High on the rock, this bird is sitting in its nest.

This is the biggest rock on Earth. You can see it from space!

I'm not kidding!

Red, Redder, Reddest

In this canyon, the sand is **red**.

People walk between the red rocks.

The sand is even redder in this place!

The oldest dunes are the reddest.

CHECKING FOR MEANING

1. What sort of plants can live in the hottest place on Earth? *(Literal)*
2. What sort of dunes are the reddest? *(Literal)*
3. Why are the plants in the wet place glad when big drops fall? *(Inferential)*
4. Would you rather spend time in the hottest place, the wettest place or the place with the reddest sand? Why? *(Evaluative)*

EXTENDING VOCABULARY

hottest	What is the base of the word *hottest*? How does adding the suffix *est* change the meaning of the word *hot*? What is the opposite of the word *hottest*?
humid	How does it feel when the weather is humid?
drifts	What is mist doing if it drifts? What is another word that has a similar meaning to *drifts*?

MOVING BEYOND THE TEXT

1. How do we know that we can see the biggest rock from space? Who would have seen it?

2. Have you ever visited places similar to those in the book? Tell me about it.

3. What would be difficult about living in the hottest place in the world?

4. What is it like where you live? Is it hot? Is it wet? Are there any big or red things nearby?

TIME TO WRITE

Compare two places in the book and explain how they are different. Can you think of any ways that they may be the same?